Building a Strong Foundation: Making an Impact in the Lives of our Youth

MLK Nation Exposure to Literature Academy, Inc.
Publishing Division

Building a Strong Foundation: Making an Impact in the Lives of our Youth

by: Minister Melvin Evans

Building a Strong Foundation:
Making an Impact in the Lives of our Youth

ISBN: 978-0-9840720-2-6
ISBN: 0-9840720-2-6

MLK Nation Exposure to Literature Academy, Inc.
Publishing Division
4703 Wheeler Road, Suite 100
Oxon Hill, MD 20745
301-839-0114

Printed in the United States of America

DEDICATION PAGE

TO MY MOTHER, HATTIE EVANS

Mother you taught me so much; you taught me that there are two sides to life. You taught me that we are free to choose either side, but that Christ's side would be victorious. (loosely translated from Luke 11:23)

For God giveth to a man that is good in his sight, wisdom , and knowledge and joys, but to the sinner he giveth travail, to gather up and to heap up, that he may give to him that which is good before God. This also is vanity and vexation of the spirit. (loosely translated from Ecclesiastes 2:26)

FOREWORD

When I left South Carolina at a young age, I had to make quite a few adjustments because city life was different from country life. Here in the city, there are more police stations, more gas stations, more stores, more parks and recreational areas and much more people.

Now in the South, we had small communities, but the principles and rules that I had learned while growing up in the South were the same as those that I would have to follow in the city. I had to realize that we have decisions to make in life and our decisions have consequences. Long ago, I decided to put God first because I knew that as long as I lived on earth, there would be rules and regulations that I would have to follow to lead a productive life.

In the South, when I was growing up the whites and blacks were divided. Many of the black people wanted to be like other people and not how nature made us. Was this self-hatred? It seemed that nobody wanted to be like God made us. As a result of this dislike of ourselves, we began to do some foolish things. Some of us began to trim off parts of our noses, others changed their hair texture and still others began to try to change our very skin color. Some of our attempts at mutation took years and lots of money, and we looked very foolish as we began to change what nature had already blessed upon us. We are a very beautiful people of many beautiful colors, but we were foolish and did not recognize our beauty.

Many of the men processed their hair by using dangerous lye that almost ate our scalps off our heads, but this lye process gave us artificial looking wavy hair which cost a lot of money to keep processed. In fact, anything that is artificial and costs a lot of time, pain and money to keep up is usually not worth it. Oh, what foolish things we did to ourselves and our bodies in order to try to look like other people. Were many African American people so ashamed of their shoe sizes, body shapes, hair and color that we were foolish enough to want to change our very appearance? What foolishness and self-hatred had we begun to assimilate? We had become a false people who were untrue to ourselves. Our women began to be artificial and paraded around in wigs, heavy make-up and tight clothes and shoes, despite going bare footed for many years. We lost perspective of ourselves and tried to be like other people; thus, we became unhappy with ourselves because we had begun to look at ourselves through the eyes of others.

My mother and other mothers had told us the truth, that there are some natural rules of nature that we cannot change, but no matter how much people teach us, there are times when we have to use our own minds and make our own decisions.

Sometimes, we have to step out and ask, "God, what shall I do"? I have worked extremely hard in my lifetime; I have crawled around on my knees to pick peas, tomatoes and other crops. While crawling around on my knees, I had to look out for snakes. I had to pick peaches for ten cents a bushel. Sometimes, we found our-selves at the mercy of other human beings who cheated us of our wages.

Ultimately after working so hard and being at the mercy of others, I realized something so sad and so profound that it changed my life most dramatically: I gradually came to the realization that I was just as good as anyone else. This realization made me feel bad and good at the same time: I felt good because I developed more respect for myself and my parents, but I felt sad because it had taken me some time to develop this new self-respect. I realized that I had spent years trying to keep up with others. Some of us had overburdened ourselves with credit company debts; we were driv-ing cars that we could not afford and wearing shoes and clothes we could not afford. I had to stop and ask myself a question. "What have I done to my own self"? Like many of us, I was caught up in a debt trap. The banks and the credit companies had me in bondage. Once more, many of us had become slaves but this time to our debts. This is no way to live. Many of us began hiding from bill collectors.

When we buy homes and have to work two jobs to buy that home, our bodies are not going to hold up for thirty years or more. First of all, we must save up our money before rushing out there to buy so much on credit. We must have a savings account even before purchasing our automobiles. Everyone should have a savings account in order to prosper. So save your money when you start your first job. Now, I know that it will be hard, but we must sacrifice and save. Also, get a good education, and learn how to invest some of the money that you earn.

DECISIONS VERSUS CONSEQENCES

- Putting God First
- Making Right Decisions
- Avoiding Foolish Decisions
- Going Against Nature
  - A. color B. nose C. feet E. changes
- Putting on The Whole Armor of God
- Avoiding Negative Peer Pressure
- Relying on The Decisions of Others Versus Relying On Jesus
- Disrespecting Our Parents or Mothers
- Following our Parents Advice
- Reading Scriptures from The Bible
- Paying Attention
- Discovering One's Own Greatness
- Planting Seeds for Our Youth to Follow
- Avoiding Drugs, Alcohol and Tobacco
- Avoiding Credit Destruction
- Saving Money for A Better Future
- Buying a Home
- Preaching God's Word
- Moving Away From Superstitions
- Learning from our History

POSITIVE IMPACTS ON OUR YOUTH

- Civilization, Laws, Regulations
- Freedoms and Constraints

A. race B. racial divisions C. unjust laws D. Southern Life and its hardships

- Consequences of Foolish Choices

A. results B. Going against Nature -color, nose, feet, hair and lye, make-up, changes from foolishness C. diseases of the mind and body

- Artificial versus Real
- Concerns about What Others Think
- Be True to Yourself

A. Ten Commandments B. Lies versus Truth C. Dissatisfactions D. Clothes

- Destruction of Others

A. chain gangs B. jail C. early graves

- Anchors and Spiritual Guidance

A. sins B. stubbornness C. negative advice E. positive examples F. grounded

- Rising from Shacks

A. government programs for indoor plumbing, sewer lines, and paying the bills for government projects

- Encouragement and Character Traits

CHAPTER 1
WORDS OF WISDOM

$\mathcal{C}$ity life was different from country life. When I left the South and came to the city, I had to deal with different people and a larger life. I knew that I had to learn to obey the laws of the land. I made up my mind to stick to the principles that my mother had instilled in me when I was growing up. Like I had been taught, I decided to put God first and to learn to deal with many different people. In order to live well and prosper, young people or youth must learn to follow good principles.

I came up under segregation, but I questioned some of its rules. I observed many things as a young man: many of the people with whom I grew up tried to change themselves, their natural selves. It seems that many of us were dissatisfied with our natural selves, and we wanted to change our very nature. Were we trying to be like other races? Now, I want youth to know that some things that we do to our bodies will kill us. For example, some of us attempted to change our hair texture and used lye to straighten or process it. We used greasy rags and paid a lot of money to process our hair or make it wavy. Today, I wonder if it was worth it to pay all of that money to burn our scalps with lye soap in order to make our hair appear to be wavy.

In the South, many people went bare footed which caused many people to have big feet. When we walked around for months at a time with no shoes on, it causes our feet to expand and grow larger. Many of us became ashamed of our shoe sizes because walking bare footed had caused our feet to grow larger. In this fashion, many of us grew dissatisfied with own natural appearances, and many of us in our dissatisfaction with self-became false and depended on artificial or imitation things such as wigs, tight clothes, heavy male-up and tight shoes that hurt our feet.

Many African-American women worked long and hard to make their daughters look good. In many instances, both parents tried to help their children get ahead; oftentimes, they were so busy working they forgot to try to teach their children to be grateful for what they had. Oftentimes, their children did not realize that their parents had to make big sacrifices in order to keep them fed and clothed.

Even today, young people have to realize that no matter how many college degrees that they have or may possess; they still have to obey the laws of the land. I myself am a self-taught man; I have studied many books, reading and rereading them until, I was sure that I would be able to pass the tests that I would be given at school or even later in life. I have made many sacrifices for my family and discovered that in life, we have to be real and let nature take its course.

The Bible teaches us that we can be in the world but not of the world. In our country and in other countries, there are many rules and regulations. As law-abiding citizens, we must obey these rules and regulations in order to prosper. Many of us, black Americans, it appeared didn't want to be like God fixed us. Some of us began using different skin creams that would change our skin color because we were not satisfied with the way that God created us or our skin colors, and we tried to change that. Like I said before, we have done a lot of foolish things. Bad things just don't come on us overnight. There are many things that we do to our bodies that will kill us or drive us to early graves. If there is anything that we do to ourselves that is going to cost us, we need to stop and think: am I going to be able to spend this money and keep this up?

Since going without shoes made many of us have very large feet, why didn't we buy shoes to keep our feet from expanding. The simple truth is many of us did not have the money to buy shoes. Isn't it foolish to worry about what others or someone else is going to say about us? Today, many people are wearing false things. Many men have been fooled by women who are all made-up instead of being real. These women wear wigs, tight clothes and lots of make-up. Later, when we get that woman alone and she begins to take off all of the fake stuff, she doesn't even look like the same woman. Sometimes, we have to get loose and not be bound by artificial clothes, tight shoes, artificial hair and tons of make-up.

The majority of time, some people are just not satisfied and cannot accept the truth, but in my lifetime, I have learned that the truth will set us free. Often, we have to make our own decisions; I began to have to make my own decisions when I turned seventeen years old. This was even before I left home. This is also when we have to apply the rules that our parents have taught us. Practicing the golden rule will take us far in life. No matter what positions we may hold in life, we cannot do anything that we want to do that is wrong because if we are doing wrong, eventually, we are going to get caught and have to pay the consequences. Then we might have to go before a judge in a courtroom and face a jury.

I have cousins who have done foolish things, and they have paid the ultimate price: court systems, prison systems and early graves. Think before you do anything foolish. In this world, we must seek spiritual guidance, and it is best, if we learn this at an early age. When we grow up, we need to have someone help us by building a solid foundation on which we can stand. Many of our mothers and fathers have blessed us by giving us this solid foundation. We are their seeds, and as their seeds we are able to weather any storm because our foundation is very strong.

When I came up from the South, things were very different. I had to adjust to a larger environment. There were more stores, police stations, restaurants and schools. In the South, I had lived in a much smaller community, but I found out that the same rules and principles that applied there applied in the city. Sometimes, we just have to get loose. I find that in many instances many people are simply not being true to themselves.

Oftentimes, they don't even want to hear the truth. When I was growing up, my mother taught me the right rules. It was a necessary skill because at sometime in our life, we have to make our own decisions. Young people must learn early on that have got to obey the rules and regulations of the land. This means that they have to apply and obey the principles of the Bible. It doesn't matter how many college degrees that they get; they have to learn to obey. There are a lot of people who could have been great leaders but who are now in jail or in early graves from doing foolish things. I, myself, am proud to say that I have never been in jail. So many of our youth today are in jail, prison, or dead from listening to their peers and doing foolish things.

Young people must realize that when they do wrong things, they are going to have pay the consequences. I myself have cousins who are dead or in jail from doing foolish things. Before young people go out on their own, they must make sure that they have put on the whole armor of God. God has given every child who comes on this earth a mother and a father even if they were created from a sperm donor or donated eggs. Even if they were given away as babies, they had a mother and a father. What if a child was given away as a baby? Children who have been abandoned have Jesus who becomes their mother and their father. Jesus puts people on earth who help children who have been abandoned by their parents. There are many organizations run by people of God who help children, but we can all help them.

Children need parents to mold and guide them while they are young. There is an old parable which says that when an old tree is blown over it is hard to straighten up. A rooted and grounded foundation is very important; our youth must be rooted and grounded and have a solid foundation because many earthly temptations will come against them. It is always important to remember what our parents taught us when we are tempted. We must keep ourselves straight and think because some people will tell us the wrong things deliberately to see if we will do these foolish things. If we do foolish things, our false friends will talk about us and laugh at us for being so foolish. When your friends pressure you to do something foolish or wrong, have a mental flashback that will keep you go straight. Ask yourself, " Is my friend saying this to me just to see if I am stupid enough to do it, even though I know that it is wrong?

Don't do the things that get you in trouble. Don't be stupid; just obey the rules or suffer the consequences. It is just that that simple--rules or consequences. Remember, the wages of sin is death. Some people want to sin and want to keep on sinning, but it is just not going to work. Oftentimes, drinking, drugging and smoking will kill you, especially if you keep on doing it. As a responsible human being, you cannot rely on the decisions of others because some things that are good for others are not good for you. Oftentimes, you have to stop and ask the Lord for his guidance. Simply stop and say, " Lord, what do you want me to do"? God answers prayers.

Perhaps God will lead you to just give a kind word or hope to another person. Encourage your friends to do the right thing. Everyone needs words of encouragement. At other times, we have to think to ourselves: Do I really want to walk around and buy a lot of stuff and run my credit cards up? Will I get myself bound by credit? I realized that I did not. One day, I stopped and thought, "What am I doing to myself?" Why am I buying a new automobile every three years on credit? Why am I going into debt? I shall have to struggle to pay these bills for years. No one else is forcing me to make these poor decisions. Who am I trying to keep up with now?

Many of us have thirty year mortgages, and we struggle to pay these mortgages? Why don't we save a set amount of money for a set amount of years before we buy a home? Why don't we use our minds and think? Tell the mortgage man, that you want a fifteen year mortgage or even a twelve year mortgage. Make some of your own financial rules.

Where I came from in South Carolina, the houses that many of us lived in were on plantations, or we had to build our own homes. When I was growing up, there weren't too many people who could afford to build their homes. There were other things that we had to do also. We had to walk to go to the spring for water for drinking, bathing, and cleaning our homes and clothes. Yes indeed, southern life was hard work.

We had to learn many adages, proverbs, rules and regulations just to stay alive. Seeds had to be sown in good soil. We learned that when an old tree was blown over in a storm, it was hard to straighten that old tree back up. Trees like people need strong foundations, and trees or people without strong foundations often perish. I came to realize that we must be rooted and grounded.

When I came to the realization that I was just as good as anyone else, I was sad. You might ask why I was sad over such a good realization. I was sad because I realized that I had done a lot of foolish things like getting into debt trying to be like other people. I had gone into debt to purchase material things that I could not afford. I drove new automobiles because I didn't want to drive old cars.

I loved my mother because my mother did a lot to support her children. She worked very hard just to feed and clothe her large family of twelve children; that is why I say that we must honor and obey our parents. Oftentimes, we do not know the sacrifices that our parents have endured just to keep us, their children, alive.

Listen young people, we cannot go out into this world and do the wrong things. Right and wrong applies to everyone. There are rules and regulations that all of us have to obey, and we must follow Jesus. Sometimes, we have to stop and ask ourselves what would Jesus do when we have a pressing problem? The Bible teaches us that faith without work is dead; therefore, we must keep the words of wisdom from the Bible in our hearts and watch as well as pray. Our black race has overcome a lot in life as we have struggled to gain educations, to get knowledge, to get jobs and to be real with ourselves and to let nature take its course. We have to be real and realize that Jesus loves all of us.

Following the golden rule can carry us a long way in life. Do you really stop and think how you treat others? Do you lie to them, spread rumors about, talk bad about them, or rejoice when you hear that they have fallen? Are you a real friend to your friends and relatives? We can hold great positions in the world and lead big companies, but that may not stop us from doing foolish things; I have got cousins who did foolish things. Some of my cousins have made many mistakes from doing foolish things. Listen to me, you must begin to stop and think; before you leave home, make sure that you wear the whole armor of God. Just about everyone has a mother and father even if he was given away at birth.

People must learn at an early age that, "Man cannot live by bread alone…." When we are rooted and grounded in a solid foundation and the teachings of our parents, we have a better chance of success in life. Let us look at our seeds. All life forms begin with seeds; some of our seeds get scattered to the wind. Some of our seeds become rooted and grounded. If we forget our righteous teachings, we will suffer the consequences of our wrong doings. Oftentimes, children and even grandchildren suffer the consequences of our sins.

I witnessed my uncle working on a chain gang for being drunk in public. I have witnessed the consequences of other people who don't follow rules. They will say, " I am just going to do this because I enjoy doing it." Consequently, they do what they want to do, but if they keep on doing wrong, it is only a matter of time before their wrong doing catches up with them. Sometimes, they may even die from alcohol, drugs, overeating and sexual diseases.

Do you remember what your parents taught you when you are tempted to do wrong? If you are tempted to do wrong, you must remain straight. You must stop and think because some people will tell you wrongs things to test you and see if you are stupid enough to do foolish things. If you are, they will laugh at you and wonder how you could be so stupid.

Nowadays, they have developed all kinds of tests to see what substances and drugs a person has in his system. When sin comes full blown, things happen. Drinking too much alcohol will kill you sooner or later. Smoking cigarettes is going to kill you sooner or later, but many people think that they are going to dodge death.

People do many foolish things in their lives; there are some men who say that they won't get married if they can't find a woman as good as their mother. I wonder what some people are looking for these days. I do know that some people are looking for encouragement and kindness. As a youth, I had to do a lot of hard work in order to survive. I picked cotton, peaches and peas. Many times, I scrapped my knees and hurt my joints. Then, I got cheated from my wages; the scales were rigged.

It took me years to realize that I am just good as anyone else. Also, I realized that I had used credit cards and became bound by debt when I was trying to keep up with others. At this very moment, many of us are going into debt to keep up with others. We get ourselves into debt trying to impress and keep up with others. We work ourselves into early graves and overburden ourselves with crushing debt. What are we doing to ourselves? Why are we doing these foolish things to ourselves? Are we doing the math when we are buying on credit? Oftentimes, when we buy homes and cars on credit, we are overburdening ourselves with debt. Watch your spending, or you may come to regret it.

Some houses that we have lived in were unsuitable. I remember that in South Carolina government officials came and inspected many houses. They put indoor plumbing and sewage lines in for people. Some of the old people in the South were very superstitious and afraid of modern things such as central air conditioning and central heating. Many of these people refused these additions to their homes once they learned that they would get monthly bills for their sewage lines and other additions to their homes. They simply didn't want the monthly bills. Did many of them feel that they simply could not afford to pay additional bills and that they government would take their homes?

Many of these people just like my mother were very ac-customed to hard work. They were used to going miles to a spring to get water. Water for drinking, bathing and cleaning was carried from springs to the homes. My mother had to scrub clothes on a scrub board. She also made and used lye soap made out of hog bones and other ingredients. This was a powerful soap. My mother worked hard; she like a lot other black folks were dependent on white folks for hand-me-down clothes for their children. Some folks worked not for money but simply for those used, old clothes.

One of the major premises of life is put God first, and ask Him to guide you. Another major premise of life is that life has its restrictions. Stop trying to be artificial and trying to change our natural selves. Be real! Other sound principles we must learn are to obey the laws of the land.

If you are with a group of your friends and they want to do something wrong, you have to avoid that. Of course, they are going to berate you and call you names, but that is when you have to say a prayer for divine intervention. God answers prayers. Our parents cannot be with us and hold our hands, but we must believe that God will lead and guide us when we put your faith in Him. Stop and pray! You may pray silently, but pray!

Realize it when we are doing foolish things. When I was young, I used that skin cream to change my color, and that cream had me looking like a spotted cow. Why did I use that cream on my face? I used that cream because I like many of us was not satisfied with my natural skin, and I wanted to change my natural self. Now, this was utter foolishness; we wanted to change how God had made us.

Well things just don't come upon us overnight, and some of the things that we have done to our bodies come back to haunt us years later. Some of the unnatural things that we have done to ourselves and our bodies just don't go away.

Oftentimes, we have paid out a lot money to make our hair wavy and we have struggled to keep it wavy. We have used the money we could have used for shoes, clothes and other important necessities to give ourselves artificial waves. What fools we have been! Also some people would deliberately buy the wrong shoe size because they were ashamed of their big feet and a few messed up their feet for life. As a young man, I went barefooted for long periods of time. One day I went barefooted to the beach and the sand felt so good on my feet; however, I had to wear shoes in the city because some streets were full of glass and other harmful objects.

There are some people who simply cannot accept the truth. They listen to the opinions of other too often, but they are going to have to wake up and realize that one day, they will have to make their own decisions. They won't be able to turn to anyone else and ask them to decide for them. They will have to apply the rules that their mothers of fathers taught and come to their own decisions. All of us must realize that we cannot get away with doing wrong things because sooner or later, we are going to get caught and have to suffer the consequences. A judge or jury will tell us what to do. When we do the wrong things, we pay dearly.

Young people before you leave home and go out on your own, make sure that you carry with you the whole amour of God. Make sure you carry with you the right principles that you were taught and carry with you spiritual guidance because you cannot live by bread alone.

CHAPTER 2
BE TRUE TO YOURSELF

*O*ld trees when blown over cannot straighten up readily; that is why we need good anchors and have strong foundations that have been built by our mothers and fathers when we were young. As we historians know, our foundations were ripped from beneath us, and we had no foundation on which to build.

In recent years, we have begun to realize that we may have been beaten, but we could not be broken. That is why when we are told by our peers to do something wrong, we must flashbacks to what our parents taught us and say, " No, I can't help you rob that gas station because I know that robbing and stealing is wrong." The Biblical rule "Thou shall not steal." will resonate in your conscience and you will not do the wrong thing and get in trouble and face a judge and jury and end up with a twenty year sentence for bank robbery. As I said before," You must obey the rules and regulations of the land.

If you keep on sinning and your sins become full blown, you are going to die because the wages of sin is death. We must realize that God gives us life. When we realize that we cannot always rely on other people, even our parents, we must rely on God. Another very important thing to realize is that we cannot rely on other people's decisions because we might not all have the same talents. For instance, I might not have the ability to sing like other people, but I might be able to encourage other people along their journey. We must realize that everyone needs a little encouragement now and then. We can give them a smile, a pat on the back and a kind word.

I can remember how I felt when I was growing up poor, barefooted and driving a plough. I was crawling around on my hands and knees, watching out for snakes and working very hard. I appreciated any kind words that were spoken to me.

In conclusion, youth should obey their parents, the rules and regulations of their nation and follow the teachings of the Bible in order to live a more prosperous and healthy life. They must work, save, and set goals for their future endeavors.

CHAPTER 3

A LESSON IN HUMILITY

*T*he haughty man climbed slowly out of his bright, new Lexus to purchase gas. His knees pained him, but he was on his way to the bank to get some cash; he spotted the bum at the station and thought, " another beggar.", but the bum was watching him closely too. Suddenly, the bum said, "May I help you?" This highly insulted the haughty man because he felt that this bum was calling him old and helpless. At 68, he felt far from helpless, yet he knew that his knees had taken a beating from years of earlier farm work. Now, he was a highly respected professor at a junior college; but over the years, he had forgotten his humble beginnings and now he felt as if this bum was saying," Let me help you old man." "I don't need your darn help. " replied the haughty man as he walked over to the station to charge his gas because his credit card reading said, "see attendant."

The bum started cursing the haughty man out, but the haughty man got loud too and sprouted a few curse words back at the bum. Then the bum who was smaller and younger than the haughty man cursed some more and said to the haughty man," You insulted me and you had no right to do that," I just asked you if you needed any help. You certainly don't have any God in you to insult me like that." The haughty man, however, felt like he had been insulted first. When the bum looked at the haughty man, the haughty man looked back at the bum and saw him in a new light; he saw a fellow human being who needed a hand-out and perhaps a word of encouragement and kindness. The haughty man said, " I felt insulted when you implied I needed your help." In his mind he thought, what can this bum do for me? The haughty man knew that he was respected daily. After all, he was a respected teacher and a successful self-man made man, yet now he felt as if this bum had insulted him by asking him if he could help him. All the while, he knew that the bum was only seeking his help and was looking to him for money.

Now, the bum raged on cursing and telling the haughty man off until he hit a cord in the haughty man's heart. At last the haughty man thought, "I am a self-made man, but I am not rich. I have money to pay my bills and help my grandchildren, but I am sick of these beggars approaching me daily. If I give them money, I won't have enough for myself besides, I am afraid to pull out my wallet at times." Then, the haughty self-made man thoughts flashed back to his college days. Who had given him his college scholarships that gave him a leg up? Who had helped him when he was in need? Now that he had risen a little high than the beggar, how dare he look down on this 'bum.' Here but for the grace of God, am I thought the haughty man as he reached inside his pocket and pulled out two dollars and give it to the 'bum'. Then he said, "I am very sorry that I insulted you, but I thought you had insulted me first. Things will get better for you the haughty man said to the beggar. The beggar looked so pleased on hearing these kind words. There

now, he had given the beggar some money, but even more importantly, he had given him a few encouraging words but the haughty
man had been given even more. The haughty man had learned a
very valuable lesson; he had learned that, " No man makes it on
this earth alone, no man, and at times, we all need someone to lean
on." The haughty man had been taught a lesson in humility: he had
learned that no man is a 'bum' and often people just need to "hear
a kind word." People are not working together for the betterment
of others. We who are ministers, teachers, politicians, community
leaders, and others who are here to help others lead and live better.

EPILOGUE

When many African Americans left the South for various cities, most faced a great cultural shock because life in the country and life in the cities was very different. Most people left the South unprepared for city jobs, but many principles of life remained the same, despite the region. Just as the people who left the South had to readjust to city life, our youth have to do many things to adjust to living in our highly advanced technological society.

Our youth must prepare themselves for "living the good life." Young people must take advantage of school and start taking their educations seriously. They must pay attention in school and study hard to pass their exams and earn good grades so that they can prepare for college and get a college degree. They might even aspire to own their own businesses and create jobs for others. The opportunities are there, but young people must prepare themselves to take advantage of these opportunities. They must follow the right principles of life and put on the whole armor of God. Young people knew to know that freedom does not mean doing everything that they want to do. They cannot do foolish things and think that they will get away with doing them.

It is important that adults and young people learn that rules are made to be obeyed, and that in most instances, their parents have sought to provide them with a solid foundation upon which they must continue to build. They are cautioned not to listen to bad advice because sometimes others will give them foolish advice. Most importantly, they need to know that once they are employed, they must get to work on time. They must pray and seek spiritual guidance in times of stress. Another important thing to remember is that they are just as good as others, and that they do not have to be like others. They must be real; they don't have to be concerned with what others think about them. They needed to focus on Jesus, and love and respect their mothers and fathers. I cannot overly stress, that they must remember that what goes around comes around. Another important thing to remember is that they must save for the material things they want in life and not to overburden themselves with debt. They must remember to save a little money each pay period and to make saving a habit.

Young people must avoid drugs, tobacco and too much alcohol. They don't need those substances in their bodies. They must also avoid going to jails and prisons. Too many of our youth are destroying themselves and being sent to prisons at an early age. They do not need to be locked up like animals in cages. Our youth must be grounded and rooted in Biblical principles and doing the will of God.

Very importantly, youth must begin to plant their seeds in the garden of life early. It is never too early to begin to set goals for their futures and even for the futures of the children they will have someday. They might ask, "What are seeds?" Well, I say seeds are their words, gestures, actions, time, money and any other natural useful resources that can benefit mankind. Seeds are the harvest of life or the rewards of God's blessings. I say to ministers, teachers, preachers, farmers, businessmen, firemen, policemen, reporters, doctors, lawyers and Native American chiefs, we must all unite to help build a strong, solid foundation for our youth, and of course, our ministers and political leaders must guide us in the right direction.

In concluding, when we guide our youth and impact their lives in a positive direction, we are doing the right things for them are our future. If just one American child is planning for his funeral and not setting goals for his life, that is one too many. Let us help our young people survive and survive well in life.

The End

ABOUT THE AUTHOR

Minister Melvin Evans was born and raised on a farm in Kenshaw, South Carolina where he attended various schools in the area. When he was nine years of age he was required to plow the fields as part of his chores. He used a mule to plow the fields; one of the major problems young Melvin would encounter was the danger of plowing up snakes. Now, he was very afraid of snakes. On one occasion a snake got into his home and terrorized the entire family. Country life was all about working the land to make a living. For awhile, he picked peaches for 10 cents a bushel, picked peas for 35 cents for 100 pounds and picked cotton for 75 cents a pound. Minister Melvin Evans worked hard as a child, and often worked for 75 cents a day.

At 17 years of age, he left South Carolina and moved to Greensboro, North Carolina. There Melvin worked for a construction company, a Woolworth Store and North Carolina A&T College. The North Carolina A & T college students held sit-ins occurred doing the 1960's at the same Woolworth Store were he worked. He could sense the changes coming to America as African Americans demonstrated for their civil rights.

Later, he moved to Pittsburg, Pennsylvania and worked at the local YMCA before moving to Washington, DC and securing a job at The Pentagon. After applying good life principles and acquiring additional job skills, Mr. Evans made the decision to go to work for The C&P Telephone Company, later known as Bell Atlantic and now Verizon where he retired as a building engineer after 32 years of service. He received an award from The Public Affairs and Administration Department in recognition of outstanding attendance for 1980. He earned his award and made the attendance honor roll for no absences for that entire year. Throughout his employment, Melvin Evans earned many awards and commendations for his work ethics.

When he was young, Minister Evans always wanted a bicycle, but his mother was not able to buy him one. Growing up as children, his brothers and sisters would often make their own wagons, fish hooks, bicycles and anything else that they wanted to play with or for entertainment. Young Melvin also loved shooting marbles. Now like the youth whom he wishes to inspire, he says, "Hold fast to dreams. .." At the age of 40 not forgetting his love for the bicycle, he bought himself a bicycle. He feels that it is never too late to fulfill one's dreams.

Presently, Mr. Evans is in the ministry and has written a stupendous book about his growing up in poverty and overcoming many obstacles by using Godly principles and good common sense. He is very proud of the fact that he has never gone to jail. This is very important for youth to ponder because many young men are imprisoned today and destroying their futures. It is more difficult for ex-convicts to integrate back into society. They get few job interviews and fewer good paying jobs. Oftentimes, they have learned no new skills in prison because most prisons are human waste lands. Everyone talks about common sense but few people write about it in a very practical sense as Minister Evans has. From his words of inspiration, one feels his reliance on God; he uses God as a guide for his daily life and follows The Golden Rule as he teaches us to use Bible principles in our daily lives. He also admonishes us to honor our mothers and fathers and to lead prosperous, sensible lives and not allow ourselves to use credit to drag us down. Credit, he believes is another form of slavery. He believes that people should save, save and save to buy the things they want.

Minister Evan's ultimate goal is to give youth and others hope, sound advice and to help parents, teachers, ministers, sports leaders, politicians and other leaders to obey the rules and regulations of God and man and to serve as role-models for our youth. He feels that community leaders should serve as community resource people and minister to all youth regardless of race, creed or religion.

ADVICE ABOUT AVOIDING FOOLISH DECISIONS

Be true to yourself; be happy with your natural self and stop relying on other's opinions. When we are disobeying the rules, eventually there will be some authority figure who will tell us what to do like a judge and jury because we have to obey the rules of the society in which we live.

It is very important that we think for ourselves and carry with us the whole armor of God. Let us look at big trees in a storm. When big trees are blown down, they can not spring back up like young trees that are rooted and grounded in a strong foundation. Youth grounded in a strong foundation can spring back up like young trees. All of us need solid foundations to weather storms; continuous use of drugs and alcohol are destroyers of mankind. When people drink or drug a lot, they destroy relationships, marriages and careers. Sometimes, they listen to people who tell them things that don't mean them any good. People have to learn to think for themselves and make their own decisions. They must ask themselves, " Am I making a good decision"? They must stop doing foolish things. They must avoid making bodily changes to look like other people. We must teach our youth respect and caring, not only about themselves, but about other people.

Many of our parents have worked extremely hard scrubbing dirty clothes on scrub boards and pressing shirts like a laundry. We have to rely on God's help because nobody, not even our parents, will be able to hold our hands everyday We have to make daily decisions with God's help. Life is about decision making. Are we making good decisions about our education, careers, and daily living? Are we applying the golden rule and making others feel better about themselves? Are we showing others respect? Are we avoiding things that will put us at the mercy of others? Are we as a society giving guidance to all youth? If not, we as a people must begin to do so. According to General Colin Powell who always takes time to aid youth, all adults should give guidance to help our young people make solid decisions in life.

FIVE STEPS TO A SOLID FOUNDATION

> Faith in God
> Obey the rules, regulations and laws of the land
> Honor your mother and father
> Be true to self
> Make good decisions

CONTACT THE AUTHOR

Minister Melvin Evans
301-518-4553

CPSIA information can be obtained at www.ICGtesting.com
Printed in the USA
BVOW020617240513

321535BV00007B/137/P